FAST FACTS

*All You Need to
Keep up to
Speed*

Depression

Second edition

David S Baldwin DM FRCPsych

Senior Lecturer in Psychiatry
Clinical Neuroscience Division
Faculty of Medicine, Health and Life Sciences
University of Southampton
Southampton, UK

Robert MA Hirschfeld MD

Titus H Harris Chair
Department of Psychiatry and Behavioral Sciences
The University of Texas Medical Branch at Galveston
Texas, USA

Declaration of Independence

This book is as balanced and as practical as we can make it. Ideas for
improvement are always welcome: feedback@fastfacts.com

HEALTH PRESS
Oxford

Fast Facts – Depression
First published 2001
Second edition March 2005

Text © 2005 David S Baldwin, Robert MA Hirschfeld
© 2005 in this edition Health Press Limited
Elizabeth House, Queen Street, Abingdon, Oxford OX14 3LN, UK
Tel: +44 (0)1235 523233
Fax: +44 (0)1235 523238

Book orders can be placed by telephone or via the website.
For regional distributors or to order via the website, please go to:
www.fastfacts.com
For telephone orders, please call 01752 202301 (UK),
+44 1752 202301 (Europe) or 800 538 1287 (North America, toll free).

Fast Facts is a trademark of Health Press Limited.

A CIP catalogue record for this title is available from the British Library.

ISBN 1-903734-48-7

Baldwin, DS (David)
Fast Facts – Depression/
David S Baldwin, Robert MA Hirschfeld

Typesetting and page layout by Zed, Oxford, UK.
Printed by Fine Print (Services) Ltd, Oxford, UK.

Printed with vegetable inks on fully biodegradable and
recyclable paper manufactured from sustainable forests.

Low emissions
during production

Low
chlorine

Sustainable
forests

Introduction

Depression is undoubtedly a common disorder, and one that is often severe. For the individual, it causes significant psychological distress, reduces quality of life and is associated with an increased mortality, as a consequence of related suicide, accidents and cardiovascular disease. It may also contribute to marital and family breakdown. Depression in mothers can delay the development of their children. The economic burden on society arises not only from the direct health and social care costs, but also from the indirect costs. These encompass losses due to the reduced work productivity of patients and informal carers, and the costs of premature death due to suicide (the cause of death in approximately 10% of patients with severe, recurrent, depressive disorder).

The overall management of people with depression is often far from ideal. Stigma and discrimination make people who might be suffering from depression reluctant to present for treatment. Even after the patient presents with psychological symptoms, the recognition of depression by doctors and other health professionals is variable and often poor.

Delivery of care and treatment is rather patchy and often inadequate, and relatively few depressed patients are offered the range of pharmacological and psychological treatments shown to have value in consolidating clinical recovery and preventing a return of their depressive illness.

Primary care teams have been and will continue to be the main providers of treatment for depressed patients. Although the advantages of safer and better tolerated antidepressants have been clearly established in secondary care, this is not yet the case in primary care settings, where further prospective studies of clinical efficacy and cost-effectiveness are required.

Short-term psychological treatments have been found to be effective for depressed patients in primary care settings; however, these treatments have not been adopted extensively. Much more research into the outcome of depression in primary care is needed, with a balanced evaluation of the effectiveness and acceptability of pharmacological and psychological treatments.

Fast Facts – Depression summarizes the features, consequences, causes and treatments of the range of conditions collectively known as the 'affective' or mood disorders. Although this book is not a comprehensive tome, we trust that the information presented will benefit you and your patients with depression.

Key references

Aldridge S. *Seeing Red and Feeling Blue: The New Understanding of Mood and Emotion*. London: Century, The Random House Group, 2000.

Jamison KR. *Touched with Fire: Manic-Depressive Illness and The Artistic Temperament*. New York: Free Press, 1993.

Kasper S, den Boer JA, Ad Sitsen JM, eds. *Handbook of Depression and Anxiety*. 2nd edn. New York: Marcel Dekker, 2003.

Milligan S, Clare A. *Depression and How to Survive it*. London: Ebury Press, 1993.

Varma V, ed. *Managing Manic Depressive Disorders*. London: Jessica Kingsley, 1997.

Wilkinson G, Moore B, Moore P. *Treating People With Depression: A Practical Guide For Primary Care*. Oxford: Radcliffe Medical Press, 1999.

'Depression' covers a range of related conditions in which the primary disturbance is thought to be one of mood or 'affect'. Traditionally, this group includes the depressive disorders, mania and hypomania, and the anxiety disorders. Better delineation of the anxiety disorders together with an often selective response to treatment have led to them being considered separately from depression.* The anxiety syndromes commonly seen by the primary care provider will be briefly considered here, however, as they show extensive cross-sectional and longitudinal overlap with the depressive syndromes.

Attitudes towards depression

The public's perception. Depression is a much misunderstood condition. Repeated surveys of the general population in the UK and questionnaire surveys of members of depression 'user' groups reveal widespread public attitudes that may hinder the achievement of optimal outcomes for people with depression. Although opinion poll findings have indicated a steady increase in the proportion of the population who believe depressed patients should be treated with antidepressants, this belief is still held by only a quarter of the general public. In contrast, 'counseling' (which has uncertain efficacy in the treatment of depression of more than mild severity) and psychotherapies remain a popular choice. Most of the sampled individuals believe that antidepressants are addictive. However, more people now appear to accept that 'biological changes in the

*The second edition of *Fast Facts – Anxiety, Panic and Phobias*, by Malcolm Lader and Thomas W Uhde, will be published by Health Press Limited in 2005.

brain' can cause depression. In short, small but significant changes in attitudes towards depression have occurred over the past decade, but whether these have led to altered behavior (for example, a greater readiness to consult a doctor when troubled by psychological symptoms) is not clear.

Healthcare professionals. Misunderstandings and misgivings about depression are also widespread in the medical and related professions. For example, many doctors believe that if a patient's depression seems 'understandable', then it should not be treated. Others are unaware of the need for long-term pharmacological or psychological treatment after symptomatic improvement to prevent early relapse or later recurrence of illness.

Primary and secondary care budget holders worry about the cost of seemingly expensive new pharmacological treatments for depression, while healthcare policy makers tend to focus their attention on severe mental illness (such as schizophrenia), overlooking the fact that depression is a potentially fatal disorder. When combined with the widespread fear of mental illness, the stigma of a psychiatric diagnosis and the associated discrimination in work opportunities, these misunderstandings together serve to maintain suboptimal clinical outcomes for people with depression.

Unhappiness or depression?

Unhappiness is part of the usual human reaction to adversity, but it can also occur unexpectedly and with no obvious cause. The symptom of depressed or low mood is present when unhappiness lasts longer than expected, appears out of proportion to circumstances or seems beyond personal control. Depressed mood may occur in certain physical illnesses (such as malignancy, hepatitis or glandular fever) and as part of many different psychiatric syndromes.

Depressive disorders are characterized by low mood, reduced energy and loss of interest or enjoyment. Other common symptoms include poor concentration, reduced self-confidence, guilty thoughts, pessimism, ideas of self-harm or suicide, disturbed sleep and altered appetite. The severity of an episode varies, and can be assessed from the number, type and intensity of symptoms, and the associated impairment at work and in personal or family relationships.

Depression in primary care

The majority of depressed patients are managed by their primary care physician, and depression presenting with or without anxiety symptoms constitutes the bulk of psychiatric morbidity seen in primary care settings. In the USA, the percentage of depressed patients treated by a primary care physician increased from 50% in 1987 to 64% in 2001. In the UK, each primary care physician diagnoses about 100 depressed patients a year (Table 1.1), but considerably more will not present for treatment, or will not be recognized as suffering from

TABLE 1.1

Depression among patients seen by a UK primary care physician*

Patient characteristics	Incidence of depression (cases/year unless otherwise stated)
Undiagnosed and untreated depressed patients	400
Diagnosed and treated depressed patients	100
Patients referred to a psychiatrist	10
Episodes of deliberate self-harm	3
Suicide	1 in 5 years

*Based on an average of 2500 patients.

depression. The estimated incidence of depression in an average general practice population of 2500 patients in the UK is shown in Table 1.1.

A World Health Organization (WHO) study has shown that depression is common among patients attending their primary care physician. Around 10% of patients can be classed as having a depressive episode according to the *International Statistical Classification of Diseases and Related Health Problems*, Tenth Revision (ICD-10), and a further 2% fulfill diagnostic criteria for dysthymia (a chronic mild depressive disorder). Many other patients have depressive symptoms that fall short of the diagnostic threshold for a depressive disorder. However, a significant proportion of cases of depression are missed. Patients may not recognize depression in themselves, or they may consider themselves depressed but worry about the consequences of a diagnosis of depression on employment or insurance. Others will be fearful of the potential side effects of antidepressant drugs. Doctors tend to overlook depression in the physically ill, and sometimes dismiss depression as 'understandable' when it appears to be linked to social adversity or multiple undesirable life events.

At present, it is unclear whether recognition improves the outcome of depression in primary care. Many years ago, it was shown that patients with unrecognized depression had poorer short-term outcomes for measures of low mood, reduced energy and irritability, compared with those in whom depression had been diagnosed. Subsequently, it was found that disclosure of depression in patients whose depression had not been recognized by their doctors had little effect on outcome at 6 or 12 months, largely because the doctors did not act on the information. More recently, it was shown that the introduction of a 'chronic disease management approach' (with components relating to case detection and management, and referral to specialist services),

improved recognition rates and prescription of therapeutic doses of antidepressants, although this effect was partly dependent on the patient case mix and practice resources.

Improving diagnosis. Some doctors diagnose depression with great accuracy. For others, accuracy can be improved by videotaping consultations and then gaining feedback from colleagues. Interview technique (Table 1.2) and personality can account for much of the difference in accuracy; doctors who are more accurate tend to have higher scores on scales measuring positive self-regard and responsiveness to personal needs and feelings. Of course, certain cues help with the recognition of depression, such as when patients complain of low mood or other typical depressive symptoms (Table 1.3). Other cues include repeated presentation with medically unexplained physical symptoms and a sense of despondency in the patient.

TABLE 1.2

Interviewing behavior that leads to accurate diagnosis of depression

Early in interview

Establish good eye contact

Clarify the presenting complaint

Use open followed by closed questions

Use direct questions for physical complaints

Use direct questions for psychosocial and emotional symptoms

During interview

Use an empathic style

Be sensitive to verbal and non-verbal cues

Avoid reading notes in front of the patient

Cope well with over-talkativeness by imposing structure on the consultation

Do not concentrate on the patient's previous problems

TABLE 1.3

Cues for recognizing depression

- Patient complains of being depressed
- Patient complains of other typical depressive symptoms
- Somatic symptoms present without known cause
- Patient is unduly troubled by symptoms
- Patient consults doctor without obvious change in clinical status
- Recurrent presentation of healthy children by parent
- Doctor thinks patient is depressed

Qualitative research indicates that patients worry about taking up too much of a doctor's time. This can have adverse effects on recognition and management of depression. If the physician recognizes during an initial consultation that a patient is depressed, it is often helpful to arrange to see the patient again when more time is available – perhaps by booking a double appointment within the next few days. He or she can then assess the severity of depressive symptoms and decide whether antidepressants should be prescribed and, if so, how to encourage adherence to treatment. In addition, the doctor can decide whether a psychological treatment is also required and whether referral is necessary (Table 1.4).

Once antidepressants are started, it is sensible to review patients within a few days to monitor any side effects and to encourage compliance. Depressive symptoms usually show some improvement after 2 weeks, with more improvement within 4–6 weeks and substantial improvement within 3 months. However, doctors should then conduct regular reviews to encourage compliance with continuation treatment designed to prevent relapse, and to monitor for any late-onset adverse effects. Treatment is covered in greater detail in Chapters 5 and 6.

TABLE 1.4
Criteria for referral

- Diagnosis is uncertain
- Psychotic depression
- Severe depression
- Bipolar depression
- Comorbid general medical illness or mental disorder
- Recent suicide attempt
- Patient has intrusive suicidal thoughts or marked hopelessness
- Failure to respond to an adequate course of antidepressant treatment
- Unable to tolerate side effects of treatment
- Need for specialist treatments

Major depressive disorders

The brief account of depressive symptoms given here is essentially a summary of a 'depressive episode' as described by the WHO's ICD-10 classification (Table 1.5). The American Psychiatric Association's *Diagnostic and Statistical Manual of Mental Disorders*, Fourth Edition (DSM-IV) diagnostic criteria for major depression are very similar. This type of depressive illness is common in primary care and outpatient settings. In an attempt to describe important groups of patients, the recent classification systems include a wider range of depressive disorders than those included in earlier versions. For example, both the DSM-IV classification and the ICD-10 system include dysthymia, and the ICD-10 also incorporates recurrent brief depressive disorder (RBD).

Psychiatrists see a rather unrepresentative sample of patients: the most severely ill patients and those with comorbid disorders. Therefore, the diagnostic instruments used by specialists are not always as useful for the primary care physician. It is always

13

TABLE 1.5

Simplified clinical description of an ICD-10 depressive episode*

Core symptoms

Depressed, irritable or apathetic mood

Loss of interest and enjoyment

Reduced energy

Other common symptoms

Reduced concentration and attention

Reduced self-esteem and self-confidence

Ideas of guilt and unworthiness

Bleak and pessimistic view of the future

Ideas or acts of self-harm or suicide

Disturbed sleep

Diminished appetite

General

Severity graded according to symptom burden and associated

impairment

Duration of at least 2 weeks

*Based on the ICD-10 Classification of Mental and Behavioral Disorders.
ICD-10, *International Statistical Classification of Diseases and Related Health
Problems*, 1989 Revision. Geneva: World Health Organization, 1992.

worth bearing in mind that, although many depressed patients in
primary care do not fulfill the accepted criteria for DSM-IV
major depression or an ICD-10 depressive episode (either
because their depressive illness is too mild or too short), these
patients suffer significant psychosocial impairment and restricted
quality of life, and treatment can be extremely beneficial.

Recurrent unipolar depression. Depression is usually an
intermittent condition, with recurring episodes varying in
length, severity, impairment and response to treatment.

Recurrent unipolar depression may account for up to 10% of consultations with the primary care physician. Most depressed patients are also troubled by anxiety symptoms. Indeed, in some patients, these may be prominent, with the underlying depressive symptoms being found only after direct questioning.

The presence of somatic depressive symptoms (including weight loss, feeling worst earliest in the day and early morning wakening) generally predicts a good response to antidepressant drugs. Some severely depressed patients may experience psychotic symptoms, which can predict a good response to treatment with electroconvulsive therapy (ECT).

Dysthymia was introduced into the group of mood disorders in the DSM-III classification in 1980 and is recognized in both DSM-IV and ICD-10. It is a more chronic, but symptomatically milder, depressive disorder than major depression. Although relatively little was known about dysthymia in the early 1980s, subsequent research has resulted in a more detailed understanding of its clinical features, epidemiology, comorbidity and treatment. The social and occupational impairment seen in dysthymia is similar to that seen in major depression. Accurate diagnosis of dysthymia can be difficult, largely depending on the accurate recall of symptoms by depressed patients. Simplified diagnostic criteria for dysthymia are shown in Table 1.6.

Recurrent brief depression. Community studies, involving predominantly young adults, indicate that many of those who receive treatment for depression do not fulfill the diagnostic criteria for major depression. Some of these patients experience episodes that are rather short-lived (lasting less than 2 weeks), but are otherwise indistinguishable from major depression. In a large minority, these brief episodes recur at least monthly and

TABLE 1.6

Simplified diagnostic criteria for dysthymia*

A Depressed mood for most of the day, more days than not, for at least 2 years

B Presence, while depressed, of at least two of the following:

- poor appetite or over-eating

- insomnia or hypersomnia

- low energy or fatigue

- low self-esteem

- poor concentration or difficulty making decisions

- feelings of hopelessness

C Never without symptoms listed in A or B for more than 2 months within a 2-year period

D No evidence of unequivocal major depression during the first 2 years of the disturbance

E No history of mania or an unequivocal hypomanic episode

F Not superimposed on a chronic psychotic disorder

G Not initiated or maintained by organic factors

H Causes clinically significant distress or impairment in social, occupational or other important areas of functioning

*Based on DSM-IV criteria. Reprinted with permission from the *Diagnostic and Statistical Manual of Mental Disorders*, Fourth Edition. Copyright 2000, American Psychiatric Association.

are associated with significant social and occupational impairment. The modified Zurich criteria for RBD are shown in Table 1.7. Similar descriptions are now included within the ICD-10 and Appendix B of the DSM-IV. Although brief, the discrete depressive episodes are usually severe and are sometimes associated with suicidal behavior. More research in clinical samples in primary and secondary care is needed before the diagnosis can be accepted widely.

TABLE 1.7

Zurich criteria (modified) for recurrent brief depression

- Dysphoric mood or loss of interest or pleasure
- Four of the following symptoms:
  - poor appetite or significant weight loss
  - insomnia or hypersomnia
  - psychomotor agitation or retardation
  - loss of interest or pleasure in usual activities, or decrease in sexual drive
  - feelings of worthlessness, self-reproach or excessive guilt
  - diminished ability to think or concentrate; indecisiveness
  - recurrent thoughts of death, suicidal thoughts, wishes to be dead or suicide attempts
- Duration of depressive episodes is less than 2 weeks but recurring at least monthly over 1 year
- Reduced subjective capacity at work

Seasonal affective disorder. The current criteria for seasonal affective disorder (SAD) state that there should be at least three episodes of mood disturbance in 3 separate years, of which 2 or more years are consecutive. As follow-up studies indicate that many patients with SAD develop significant non-seasonal depressive episodes, the criteria stipulate that seasonal episodes must outnumber non-seasonal episodes by more than 3:1.

Mixed anxiety and depressive disorder. The ICD-10, but not the DSM-IV, includes a subsyndromal category of mixed anxiety and depressive disorder (MADD). This should be recorded when symptoms of both anxiety and depression are present, but where neither set of symptoms, when considered separately, is sufficiently severe to justify a diagnosis of depression or of an anxiety disorder. A household survey of psychiatric morbidity in the UK found a point prevalence for MADD of 7.7%, compared with 2.1% for depressive episodes, as defined by ICD-10. The course and treatment outcome of MADD are largely unknown, but the condition is likely to be of particular relevance in primary care.

Bipolar affective disorder. Lifting of mood is part of the usual response to good fortune, but elation can also occur without any obvious cause; alternatively, it may seem excessive or too prolonged. Elation can be a feature of several psychiatric syndromes, including manic episodes, acute schizophrenic episodes and various drug-induced states. The abundant energy and increased activity of people experiencing manic episodes are usually accompanied by an exaggerated sense of subjective well-being, but many patients feel irritable and exasperated, and the euphoric mood is sometimes tinged with sadness. In some patients, irritability, agitation and hostility may be prominent, in the absence of elation. Other patients simultaneously meet the criteria for both a manic episode and a major depressive episode – this being designated a 'mixed episode' in the DSM-IV classification.

Typically, elation is reflected in excessive talkativeness (pressure of speech) and the quick succession of grandiose ideas and unrealistic plans. Impairment of judgment can lead to financial or sexual indiscretions that may ruin personal and family life. Insight into the changes in mood, activity and interpersonal relationships is usually reduced, contributing to the high compulsory admission rates for manic patients. The DSM-IV criteria for mania are shown in Table 1.8.

Depression is frequent in patients with bipolar disorder and lasts much longer than episodes of mania or hypomania. It may be indistinguishable from depression in non-bipolar patients, but symptoms of low energy, hypersomnolence and hyperphagia are

TABLE 1.8

Diagnostic criteria for mania*

- Distinct period of elation or irritability
- Three of the following:
  - overactivity
  - increased talkativeness or pressure of speech
  - flight of ideas or racing thoughts
  - inflated self-esteem or grandiosity (which may be delusional)
  - decreased need for sleep
  - distractibility
  - indiscreet behavior with poor judgment (e.g. sexual, financial)
- Marked impairment in occupational or social function

*Based on DSM-IV criteria. Reprinted with permission from the *Diagnostic and Statistical Manual of Mental Disorders*, Fourth Edition. Copyright 2000, American Psychiatric Association.

more common than in unipolar depression. The treatment for non-bipolar depression may destabilize bipolar patients, precipitating manic or hypomanic episodes. Recognition of bipolarity in patients with depression is therefore very important.

The cyclic pattern of mania and depression was previously called manic–depressive psychosis. The current term of bipolar affective disorder (or bipolar illness) is more appropriate, as many patients with marked disturbance of affect never experience psychotic phenomena, such as delusions or hallucinations.

Bipolar affective disorder has been subdivided into two categories. In bipolar I disorder, patients experience manic episodes, often requiring admission to hospital. With bipolar II disorder, a history of recurrent depressive episodes is accompanied by at least one hypomanic episode, in the absence of manic or mixed episodes.

Key points – recognizing depression

- Many primary care patients with treatable depressive disorders are not recognized as having a condition that warrants treatment.
- Doctors can be trained to adopt styles of interviewing behavior that are associated with greater accuracy in recognizing depression.
- Patients should be referred to specialist mental health services when they are suffering from severe, psychotic or comorbid depression, or when they have not responded to an adequate course of antidepressants.
- Most depressed patients also have anxiety symptoms, which may be the presenting feature: patients with significant anxiety and depression tend to have a more disabling condition and poorer prognosis.
- Some patients presenting with depressive symptoms have a family history or personal history of mania; as management of these patients is often difficult, referral to secondary care mental health services is advisable.

Key references

American Psychiatric Association. *Diagnostic and Statistical Manual of Mental Disorders*. 4th edn. Washington DC: American Psychiatric Association, 1994.

Angst J, Merikangas K, Scheidegger P, Wicki W. Recurrent brief depression: a new subtype of affective disorder. *J Affect Disord* 1990;19:87–98.

Baldwin DS. Recurrent brief depression: more investigations in clinical samples are now required. *Psychol Med* 2003;33:383–6.

Paykel ES, Hart D, Priest RG. Changes in public attitudes to depression during the Defeat Depression Campaign. *Br J Psychiatry* 1998;173:519–22.

Pollock K, Grime J. Patients' perceptions of entitlement to time in general practice consultations for depression: qualitative study. *BMJ* 2002;325:687.

Scott J, Thorne A, Horn P. Quality improvement report: Effect of a multifaceted approach to detecting and managing depression in primary care. *BMJ* 2002; 325:951–4.

Stafford RS, MacDonald EA, Finkelstein SN. National patterns of medication treatment for depression, 1987 to 2001. *Prim Care Companion J Clin Psychiatry* 2001;3:232–5.

Üstün TB, Sartorius N, eds. *Mental Illness in General Health Care. An International Study.* Chichester: John Wiley & Sons, 1995.

Wells KB, Stewart A, Hays RD et al. The functioning and well-being of depressed patients. Results from the Medical Outcomes Study. *JAMA* 1989;262:914–19.

Gender

Community surveys in industrialized societies show that about 15% of the general population report significant depressive symptoms, and some 10% of consultations in primary care settings are probably due to depressive disorders. Depression is more common in women than men, with lifetime prevalences of about 20% and 10%, respectively (Figure 2.1). Furthermore, there is good evidence that women develop more complex and severe clinical pictures, and probably a more troublesome course of illness, though men are more liable to deny or forget earlier depressive episodes. The reason for the female preponderance of depression is not fully understood.

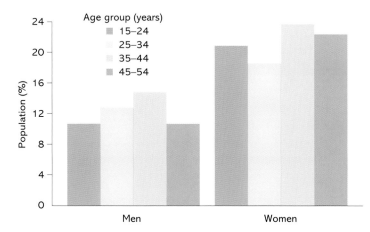

Figure 2.1 Women have a higher lifetime prevalence of major depressive disorders than men. Data from the National Comorbidity Survey. Sadock BJ, Sadock VA, eds. *Kaplan & Sadock's Comprehensive Textbook of Psychiatry*, 7th edn. Reproduced with permission of Lippincott Williams & Wilkins, copyright © 2000.

Postnatal depression. Approximately 10% of women experience significant depression in the first few months after childbirth. Many recover spontaneously, but up to half will still have depressive symptoms 6 months after delivery. Some women develop a chronic or recurrent mood disorder. About 30% of women with postnatal depression will have further postnatal depressive episodes after a subsequent pregnancy. Risk factors for the development of depression after childbirth include a history of depression before conception or during pregnancy, a poor marital relationship and lack of social support, and recent stressful life events. To these can be added severe maternity 'blues' in the first week after delivery, and irritability or poor motor control in the infant.

The hormone profiles of women with postnatal depression do not appear to differ significantly from those in non-depressed women. About 12% of women of childbearing age have thyroid microsomal antibodies in the blood; the presence of these antibodies is associated with a slightly increased risk of developing postnatal depression, regardless of whether the woman shows clinical or biochemical evidence of thyroid dysfunction. Psychosocial factors are probably more important, and risk factors may include low family income and limited social support.

Age

There is some evidence that dysthymia and minor depression are more prevalent in the elderly. By contrast, major depression appears to be less common in the elderly than in younger age groups.

Recent studies suggest a rising incidence of depression in younger age groups. Major depression in childhood is no longer considered rare, with the point prevalence in children lying in the range 0.5–2.5%. Depression is more common in adolescents than in younger children, having an average point prevalence of 2.0–8.0%. It is important not to ascribe depression in adolescents solely to developmental problems or 'teenage angst'.

Depression in children and adolescents usually arises from a combination of genetic predisposition, adverse developmental experiences and exposure to stressors. Severe depression in prepubertal patients often predicts subsequent bipolar disorder.

Social background

Although depressive symptoms are probably more frequent in the socially excluded and economically disadvantaged, depressive illness can affect people from all sections of society. Recovery from depression may be slower in socially deprived patients.

Personality types

Whether certain types of personality predispose a person to developing depression is a controversial subject. Personality assessments made while a patient is depressed are generally unreliable, as they are influenced by the anxiety, irritability and negative cognitions associated with depression. Assessments performed after recovery may also provide an inaccurate picture of the true premorbid personality, as apparent personality traits may have been affected by the depressive episode.

The best way to study the interaction between personality and mood is to perform a prospective investigation in which a group of young adults is followed over many years; needless to say, this type of research is difficult to perform and comparatively rare.

Certain personality traits may predispose an individual to mental disorders in general, rather than to depression alone. The trait most often associated with a predisposition to depression is undue interpersonal dependence (i.e. an excessive need for reassurance, support and attention from other people). This trait may not be predictive of depression in young people (aged 17–30 years), but may be associated with an increased risk in older age groups.

The presence of a clear-cut personality disorder (with persisting, maladaptive personality traits causing significant personal or interpersonal suffering) usually has an adverse effect on the clinical outcome in a patient with depression. This may be due to the difficulty in engaging in collaborative relationships with health professionals as much as it is due to the reduced opportunities for establishing wider patterns of psychosocial support at home and at work.

Low self-esteem, an obsessional personality, the experience of adversity in childhood, and maladaptive negative patterns of thinking about oneself and others, are all psychological risk factors for depression. There is also an increased risk of depression if an individual has recently experienced an excessive number of undesirable life events, particularly those involving loss (such as bereavement, divorce and redundancy). Other risk factors include persisting major difficulties such as being a lone parent, overcrowding, prolonged unemployment, poverty, and lack of social support or intimacy. It seems probable that vulnerability factors, such as the lack of an intimate confiding relationship, or caring for three or more children under the age of 15 years at home, confer a predisposition to depression when coupled with threatening life events or chronic social stress.

Genetic factors

Genetic influences are most marked in patients with severe depressive disorders and somatic symptoms. Indeed, the risk of depression in first-degree relatives of such patients has been shown to be increased in all studies, and is independent of environmental effects (in less severe forms of depression, environmental factors appear to be relatively more important).

Potential genetic markers for affective disorders have been localized to chromosomes X, 4, 5, 11, 18 and 21. Some of these sites have been linked to the pathophysiology of depression; for example, two of the putative markers on the long arm of chromosome 5 contain candidate genes contributing to the receptors for norepinephrine (noradrenaline), dopamine, γ-amino-butyric acid and glutamate. Approximately 25% of cases of bipolar illness in multiply affected families may be linked to a locus near the centromere on chromosome 18, and 20% may be linked to a locus on the long arm of chromosome 21. It is thought that most genes predisposing to bipolar depression can also predispose to unipolar disorders (Figure 2.2).

Although these findings are encouraging, it seems increasingly clear that no single genetic abnormality could account for more than a small proportion of all affective disorders. Much research

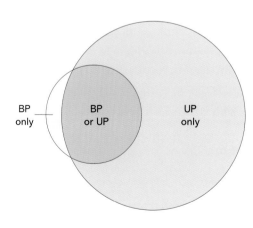

Figure 2.2 This model for the relationships between genes suggests that most genes for bipolar disorder (BP) can also predispose to unipolar disorders (UP). Thus, a subset of those with unipolar disorder may also predispose to bipolar disorder.

is underway to identify genetic markers predictive of response to pharmacological treatment.

Neurotransmitter disturbances

Preclinical research and the response of depressed patients to antidepressant treatment suggest that abnormalities in the levels or functions of the neurotransmitters serotonin (5-hydroxytryptamine, 5-HT), norepinephrine (noradrenaline) and dopamine have an important role in the pathophysiology of depression. The evidence is substantial but not yet conclusive.

Serotonin. Many aspects of serotonergic neurotransmission are altered in patients with major depression, though some of these abnormalities (such as increased numbers of platelets and brain 5-HT_2 receptors) may be linked to suicidal or impulsive behavior, rather than to the depressive syndrome itself.

Animal studies indicate that serotonin is intimately involved in the regulation of the sleep–wake cycle, appetite, sexual behavior and aggression. From neuroendocrine studies, depression appears to be associated with decreased neurotransmission at postsynaptic 5-HT_{1a} receptors; this appears to be the site at which many of the antidepressants act.

Some of the serotonergic changes seen in depressed patients may result from cortisol hypersecretion. Depression is associated with increased 24-hour adrenocorticotropic hormone (ACTH) levels, as well as elevated urinary and plasma cortisol. Exogenous administration of ACTH leads to a greater release of cortisol while the patient is depressed, suggesting a state-dependent oversensitive adrenal gland.

Depression can be associated with enlargement of the adrenal glands, which shrink in size following adequate

27

treatment. Treatment with corticotropin-releasing factor antagonists has been found to be efficacious in a small study of depressed inpatients.

Norepinephrine. Abnormalities of noradrenergic (and dopaminergic) neurotransmission may be as important as those affecting the serotonergic system. In experimental animals, norepinephrine plays a major role in maintaining arousal and drive, and in the mediation of stress responses.

Although there is no consistent change in noradrenergic receptor function in patients with depression, down-regulation of β-1-adrenoceptors by antidepressant drugs may underlie the treatment response. The availability of selective norepinephrine reuptake inhibitor antidepressant drugs should allow further exploration of the role of noradrenergic abnormalities in depressive illness.

Dopamine. Dopaminergic dysfunction has been reported in psychotic and bipolar depression, seasonal affective disorder and depression associated with Parkinson's disease. Antidepressants may resolve anhedonia (the inability to experience pleasure) and loss of drive by increasing the sensitization of dopamine D_2 and D_3 receptors.

The antidepressant sertraline has some dopamine reuptake inhibitory properties, and dopamine metabolism is altered during administration of antidepressants that inhibit monoamine oxidase, such as phenelzine.

Epidemiology by disorder

Dysthymia. The lifetime prevalence of dysthymia varies between 1% and 12%. All epidemiological studies have found higher rates in women than in men; the average female:male ratio in these studies is in the range 1.5–2.5. There is some evidence that dysthymia and minor depression are more prevalent in the elderly. By contrast, major depression appears to be less common in the elderly than in younger age groups.

Recurrent brief depression. Although it appears to be common in the general population, there has been relatively little research into the epidemiology of RBD. In the Zurich study, 14.6% of the population had fulfilled criteria for RBD by the age of 35 years. The WHO primary care study found a point prevalence of 5.2% for 'pure' RBD, together with a rate of 4.8% for RBD associated with other depressive disorders. Other studies have reported 1-year prevalence within the range 4–8%.

Seasonal affective disorder. Seasonal variations in mood are much described (particularly with worsening of mood in winter months), but epidemiological studies show little consistency regarding which season shows a peak in the number of people with depression. Retrospective investigations have found peak incidences of depressed mood in autumn, winter, spring and even late summer.

Although the concept of SAD has gained some recognition in both the ICD-10 and DSM-IV classifications, there is little epidemiological support for it being considered as a separate depressive disorder. Some epidemiological studies suggest a relationship between latitude and the prevalence of SAD, with the disorder being more common in more northern latitudes.

Bipolar affective disorder is probably more common than previously thought. Community surveys in industrialized countries indicate that the lifetime risk for bipolar I disorder is about 1%, but the wider spectrum of bipolar illness may affect as much as 9% of the population. Similar rates are seen in other cultures where, like depression, rates of bipolar disorder are higher in urban areas. Bipolar illness is equally prevalent among men and women, but there are gender differences in the course of the illness. In men, depressive and manic or hypomanic episodes occur with equal frequency, whereas in women, depressive episodes tend to predominate. Women are also more likely to exhibit rapid cycling illness. The mean age of onset is 21 years, which is earlier than for major depression. There is no convincing association with any particular social class.

There is no identifiable single cause of bipolar affective disorder; like unipolar depression, individual episodes usually result from a combination of familial, biological, psychological and social factors. The genetic 'loading' for bipolar illness is greater than that for unipolar depression. For example, the concordance rate for bipolar disorder among monozygotic (identical) twins is approximately 70%, whereas rates of major depression in studies of adult twins range from 13% to 28% among dizygotic twins and from 53% to 69% among monozygotic twins. Despite these findings, attempts to identify definite genetic markers for the condition have not yet been successful.

As in unipolar depression, abnormalities in the level or function of serotonin and norepinephrine may be important. As mania can be provoked by dopamine-releasing psychostimulants such as cocaine and amphetamine, manic episodes may be associated with overactivity in dopamine pathways within the brain. Depressed bipolar patients may be more likely than unipolar patients to respond to dopamine-enhancing agents such as bromocriptine or L-dopa. Manic episodes occurring after childbirth have been linked to abnormalities in the release of growth hormone that follows experimental challenge with dopamine-releasing investigational compounds.

Although psychosocial factors, particularly family dynamics, are undoubtedly important in influencing the course of bipolar illness once it is established, a causative role remains unclear. Studies of the impact of adverse life events have produced contradictory findings, though bereavement can be a precipitant for a manic relapse. Many relapses (both manic and depressive) can be linked to previous non-adherence to treatment with mood-stabilizing drugs.

Key points – epidemiology and etiology

- The lifetime prevalence of depression in women (around 20%) is approximately twice that found in men.
- Approximately 10% of women experience significant depressive symptoms after childbirth, but these seem related more to psychosocial than to hormonal factors.
- Disturbances in serotonergic and noradrenergic function are thought to have an important causative role in the development of depression, but may themselves result from disturbances in endocrine function.
- It is unlikely that single genes are responsible for the predisposition to (or development of) depression, but the response to treatment may be affected by pharmacogenomic factors.
- Depression is common in adolescence, and should not be ascribed solely to developmental problems or 'teenage angst'.
- Bipolar spectrum disorders are frequent in the general population, affecting up to 9% of people.

Key references

Brown GW, Adler Z, Bifulco A. Life events, difficulties and recovery from chronic depression. *Br J Psychiatry* 1988;152:487–98.

Cooper PJ, Murray L. Course and recurrence of postnatal depression: evidence for the specificity of the diagnostic concept. *Br J Psychiatry* 1995;166:191–5.

Hazell P. Depression in children. *BMJ* 2002;325:229–30.

Holmes C, Lovestone S. The molecular genetics of mood disorders. *Curr Opin Psychiatry* 1997;10:79–83.

Nemeroff CB. Recent advances in the neurobiology of depression. *Psychopharmacol Bull* 2002;36 (suppl 2):6–23.

Sadock BJ, Sadock VA, eds. *Kaplan & Sadock's Comprehensive Textbook of Psychiatry*, 7th edn. Philadelphia: Lippincott Williams & Wilkins, 2000.

Solomon DA, Keller MB, Leon AC et al. Multiple recurrences of major depressive disorder. *Am J Psychiatry* 2000;157:229–33.

Weiller E, Lecrubier Y, Maier W, Ustun TB. The relevance of recurrent brief depression in primary care: a report from the WHO Project on Psychological Problems in General Health Care conducted in 14 countries. *Eur Arch Psychiatry Clin Neurosci* 1994;244:182–9.

Although depression and anxiety can occur together, the extensive comorbidity of anxiety and depressive disorders is, in some respects, artifactual, resulting from a categorical approach to psychiatric diagnosis. A more dimensional approach in which, rather than counting symptoms, the severity of individual symptoms and signs is described, would reduce apparent comorbidity and might possibly be more relevant to clinical practice. A dimensional approach might also have more long-term stability, because categorical approaches to diagnosis tend to change as more becomes known about the features of individual mental disorders.

It seems clear, however, that when patients have significant coexisting depressive and anxiety symptoms, social and occupational impairment and reliance on healthcare resources are increased. Furthermore, the prognosis is generally not as good; symptoms tend to persist and the risk of suicidal behavior may be increased. These associations may themselves result from the somewhat poorer response of patients with coexisting depression and anxiety to traditional pharmacological and psychological treatment approaches. However, many recent studies with selective serotonin reuptake inhibitors (SSRIs) and other antidepressant drugs suggest that the presence of marked anxiety or agitation in depression does not impede the response to treatment.

Anxiety

Anxiety is a normal response to threatening or stressful events and is usually transient and controllable. It probably functions as an 'alarm' mechanism to prepare an individual for a physical response to perceived danger ('fight or flight'). By convention, a distinction is made between the psychological symptoms of anxiety and the various physical symptoms, most of which are attributable to autonomic arousal (Table 3.1). Anxiety symptoms are accorded clinical significance when they:

- are abnormally severe
- are unusually prolonged
- occur in the absence of stressful circumstances
- impair physical, social or occupational functioning.

At any one time, clinically significant anxiety affects 5–7% of the general population and 25% or more of patients in medical settings. The findings of the National Comorbidity Survey in the USA suggest that the lifetime prevalence of anxiety disorders

TABLE 3.1

Features of anxiety

Psychological	Physical
• Fear and apprehension	• Increased muscle tension
• Inner tension and restlessness	• Tremor
	• Sweating
• Irritability	• Palpitations
• Impaired ability to concentrate	• Chest tightness and discomfort
• Increased startle response	• Shortness of breath
• Increased sensitivity to physical sensations	• Dry mouth
	• Difficulty swallowing
• Disturbed sleep	• Diarrhea
	• Frequency of micturition
	• Loss of sexual interest
	• Dizziness
	• Numbness and tingling
	• Faintness

may be as high as 28.7%. Anxiety disorders in adolescence and early adult life may presage the later development of depressive disorders.

Differential diagnosis. The distinction between 'normal' responses to threat and 'abnormal' anxiety disorders is, to some extent, arbitrary, as there is probably a continuum from personal distress to psychological disorder. However, reliable diagnostic criteria such as those within DSM-IV and ICD-10 can aid recognition and treatment.

Excluding general medical illness. As there are many somatic symptoms of anxiety, differentiating it from general medical illness can be challenging. Anxiety symptoms may be mistaken for features of general medical illness, which can sometimes lead to unnecessary medical intervention. This is particularly likely if patients experience discrete episodes of paroxysmal severe anxiety (panic attacks), in which distressing physical symptoms are often accompanied by catastrophic thoughts of death or collapse.

The history or physical examination may reveal features suggestive of an anxiety disorder in patients with, for example, caffeinism or drug withdrawal, hyperthyroidism, hypoglycemia, paroxysmal tachycardia, complex partial seizures (temporal lobe epilepsy) or pheochromocytoma. These physical disorders must be considered before a firm diagnosis of anxiety disorder can be made.

Anxiety and depressive symptoms usually occur together. Some patients will therefore fulfill the criteria for 'mixed anxiety and depressive disorder' if each syndrome is relatively mild. However, when symptoms are more severe, patients can be regarded as having coexisting or comorbid anxiety and depressive disorders.

Common anxiety disorders

Generalized anxiety disorder is characterized by unrealistic or excessive anxiety and worrying that is persistent (lasts more than 6 months) and is not restricted to particular circumstances (i.e. it is free-floating). Other common features include:

- apprehension, with difficulty in concentrating, inner tension and worries about future misfortune
- motor tension, with restlessness, tremor and headache
- autonomic anxiety, with excessive perspiration, dry mouth and epigastric discomfort.

The disorder is twice as common in women as in men, and the lifetime prevalence in the general population aged 15–54 years may be as high as 5.1%. It tends to follow a fluctuating but prolonged course, and is often associated with life events and environmental stress. There is substantial comorbidity with depression, other anxiety disorders and physical illness.

The most important differential diagnosis is depressive illness. To establish whether depression is present, patients should be questioned carefully about symptoms such as loss of interest and a reduced sense of pleasure, loss of appetite and weight, diurnal variation in mood, and early morning waking. When significant depressive symptoms are present, the patient should receive treatment for depression and specific therapy for the anxiety symptoms, where appropriate.

Panic disorder and agoraphobia. Panic attacks are discrete episodes of paroxysmal severe anxiety (Tables 3.2 and 3.3). If they occur regularly in the absence of any obvious precipitating cause or other psychiatric diagnosis, panic disorder can be diagnosed. Panic attacks are characterized by severe and frightening autonomic symptoms (e.g. shortness of breath, palpitations, excessive perspiration), dizziness, faintness and chest pain. Many patients believe they are in imminent

TABLE 3.2

Typical features of panic attacks

- Sudden onset
- Short duration (typically a few minutes)
- Rapidly escalating physical and psychological symptoms
- Incapacitating symptoms of breathlessness and/or palpitations
- Fear of impending death, collapse or loss of control

danger of death or collapse, and may seek urgent medical attention.

Agoraphobia may or may not accompany panic disorder. When present, the individual feels anxious about being in places or situations from which escape may be difficult or embarrassing. Typical feared situations include being outside the home, being in a crowd, standing in a queue or using public transport. These situations are either avoided or endured with marked distress, which may be lessened by the presence of a trusted companion.

Among the general population, agoraphobia can occur as an isolated condition, but in clinical samples it is invariably associated with panic disorder and often with coexisting major depression. The lifetime community prevalence of panic disorder with or without agoraphobia may be as high as 4%. The point prevalence of panic disorder in primary care settings has been estimated to be 2%.

Although some patients with recurrent, unexpected panic attacks will be found to have unrecognized physical illness (e.g. hyperthyroidism), most will be suffering from panic disorder.

Panic disorder is associated with high rates of use of general medical, emergency and psychiatric services, and is often found in patients undergoing investigation for medically unexplained

TABLE 3.3

Diagnostic guidelines for panic disorder (based on ICD-10)

- The individual experiences recurrent panic attacks that are not consistently associated with a specific situation or object and that often occur spontaneously. The panic attacks are not associated with marked exertion or with exposure to dangerous or life-threatening situations
- The panic attack is characterized by all of the following:
  - a discrete episode of intense fear or discomfort
  - starts abruptly
  - reaches a maximum intensity within a few minutes
  - lasts at least several minutes
- At least four of the following symptoms are present, including at least one autonomic arousal symptom:

  Autonomic arousal symptoms
  - palpitations or pounding heart, or accelerated heart rate
  - sweating
  - trembling or shaking
  - dry mouth (not due to medication or dehydration)

  Symptoms involving chest and abdomen
  - difficulty in breathing
  - feeling of choking
  - chest pain or discomfort
  - nausea or abdominal distress

  Symptoms involving mental state
  - feeling dizzy, unsteady, faint or light-headed
  - feeling that objects are unreal or that the self is distant
  - fear of losing control, going 'crazy' or passing out
  - fear of dying

  General symptoms
  - hot flushes or cold chills
  - numbness or tingling sensations
- The attack is not caused by a physical disease, organic mental disorder, or other condition such as schizophrenia, mood disorder or somatoform disorder

Based on the ICD-10 Classification of Mental and Behavioral Disorders. ICD-10, *International Statistical Classification of Diseases and Related Health Problems*, 1989 Revision. Geneva: World Health Organization, 1992.

physical symptoms. To avoid 'wasting' scarce healthcare resources on patients who will not benefit from these unnecessary medical interventions, it is important that all doctors are aware of panic disorder, and are able to make a positive psychiatric diagnosis rather than just excluding all possible physical conditions.

Many people who experience panic attacks or suffer from panic disorder fulfill criteria for other disorders. For example, in the WHO Collaborative Study on Psychological Problems in General Health Care, 45.6% of patients with a history of panic attacks fulfilled ICD-10 diagnostic criteria for a current depressive episode or dysthymia. Most patients with panic disorder will experience a depressive episode at some point in their lives. When compared with those with pure panic disorder, patients with comorbid panic and depression are more severely ill and more functionally impaired at home and at work; they also make greater demands on health services. The comorbid group may also be less likely to continue with psychological or pharmacological treatments, and more likely to attempt suicide.

Specific (isolated) phobias. The characteristic feature of a specific phobia is a single, discrete fear of an object (e.g. knives) or animal (e.g. snakes), a situation (e.g. flying) or a person (e.g. a dentist). To meet diagnostic criteria:
- the fear has to be marked and persistent
- exposure to the feared stimulus will cause an immediate anxiety response
- the phobic situation is either avoided or endured with significant emotional distress.

Although the lifetime prevalence of specific phobia in the general population may be as high as 11.3%, only a small proportion of sufferers seek medical treatment for their condition. Most learn to live with the phobia, though occasionally treatment is sought when lifestyle changes are necessary (e.g. a promotion at work requires increased international travel).

Social phobia (also known as social anxiety disorder) is characterized by an intense and persistent fear of being scrutinized or evaluated by other people (Table 3.4). The patient anticipates ridicule or humiliation and usually avoids social situations such as eating in public, writing in the presence of others or conversing with strangers. The feared situations may be relatively discrete (e.g. public speaking) or diffuse, involving almost all social situations outside the family circle (the generalized subtype). Social phobia usually begins in childhood or adolescence. Once established, it can lead to academic under-performance, impaired career development, financial dependence on others and the state, and difficulties in forming and maintaining interpersonal relationships. It is associated with the later development of other anxiety disorders, depression and alcohol misuse.

TABLE 3.4

Diagnostic guidelines for social phobia

- Marked fear of being the focus of attention, or fear of behaving in a way that will be embarrassing or humiliating
- Marked avoidance of the feared situations
- Anxiety symptoms are restricted to, or predominate in, the feared situations or contemplation of the feared situations
- In addition to more typical anxiety symptoms, at least one of the following must be present:
  - blushing or shaking
  - fear of vomiting
  - urgency or fear of micturition or defecation
- The symptoms cause significant emotional distress

Key points – comorbidity

- Anxiety disorders in adolescence and early adult life may presage the later development of depressive disorders.
- Some patients with recurrent unexpected panic attacks may be suffering from unrecognized physical illness (e.g. hyperthyroidism), but most will be suffering from panic disorder.
- Social phobia has a high lifetime prevalence (up to 13%) and is associated with the later development of other anxiety disorders, depression and alcohol misuse.

Social phobia is a common condition. The National Comorbidity Survey in the USA found that the 1-year prevalence among people aged 15–54 years was almost 8%, and the lifetime risk was calculated to be as high as 13.3%. The disorder is more common in women than in men. People with social phobia are less likely to marry and more likely to divorce than the general population. The prevalence is highest in people with a low socioeconomic status, probably reflecting the lower educational attainment and restricted career progression of affected individuals.

The generalized subtype of social phobia can be confused with panic disorder. In patients with social phobia, panic attacks are usually restricted to feared social situations (or anticipation of those situations), whereas in those with panic disorder, the attacks occur unexpectedly, in social encounters or when alone. Patients with social phobia have a fear of appearing foolish and awkward, whereas those with panic disorder fear that they are in imminent danger of death or losing control. When accompanied by a trusted friend, patients with panic disorder can enjoy social encounters, but patients with social phobia find that the presence of the friend makes little difference.

Other conditions to consider in the differential diagnosis of social phobia include psychosis, as many patients with schizophrenia or other psychotic illnesses avoid social encounters, and physical disorders in which fear and anxiety may be related to concerns about medical conditions (such as Parkinson's disease, benign essential tremor, stuttering, obesity or burns).

Patients with 'pure' social phobia are relatively uncommon in clinical settings. The comorbidity of social phobia with other disorders results not only in greater use of health services, but is also linked to a significantly increased risk of suicide attempts.

Key references

Baldwin DS, Peveler R. Anxiety disorders. *Medicine* 2000;28: 11–14.

Kessler RC. Comorbidity of depression and anxiety disorders. In: Montgomery SA, den Boer JA, eds. *SSRIs in Depression and Anxiety: Perspectives in Psychiatry*, vol 8. Chichester: John Wiley, 1998:81–99.

Kessler RC, McGonagle KA, Zhao S et al. Lifetime and 12-month prevalence of DSM-III-R psychiatric disorders in the United States: results from the National Comorbidity Survey. *Arch Gen Psychiatry* 1994;51:8–19.

Piccinelli M. Comorbidity of depression and generalised anxiety: is there any distinct boundary? *Curr Opin Psychiatry* 1998;11:57–60.

Suicide is the sixth most common cause of death in the general population of the UK (after heart disease, cancer, respiratory disease, stroke and accidents); in the 15–44-year-old age group, it is the third most common cause of death.

Although suicide rates in England and Wales have declined over the past 10 years, there are still about 4000–5000 suicides annually; of these, 400–500 involve overdoses of antidepressant drugs. Men have a considerably higher risk of suicide than women (Figure 4.1).

In the USA, suicide accounts for approximately 30 000 deaths, or 1% of all deaths, each year. Suicide ranks 11th among the causes of death in the USA and is the third

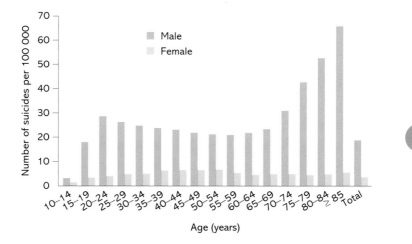

Figure 4.1 The suicide rate in the USA in 1994 according to age and sex. From Hirschfeld RMA, Russell JM. *N Engl J Med* 1997;337:910–15.

leading cause of death among those aged between 15 and 24 years.

Many countries have set targets for reducing suicide rates, often within health policy documents, and have also embarked on professional training exercises designed to improve the detection of those at particular risk.

High-risk groups

Two particular groups of patients at significantly increased risk of suicide are those with a history of suicide attempts and those recently discharged from psychiatric inpatient care.

A recent meta-analysis found that the lifetime risk of completed suicide in those who had previously attempted suicide is 40 times greater than in someone with no history of suicide attempts. This is higher than the risk attached to any particular psychiatric disorder, including major depression, or to alcoholism.

Approximately 10–15% of patients in contact with health services after a suicide attempt will eventually die by suicide, the risk being greatest in the first year after an attempt.

A combination of accurate identification of individuals with persisting risk and more assertive follow-up strategies may in theory prove effective for reducing completed suicide rates. This is an area in which the primary care provider is likely to have an important role. However, there is currently little evidence to suggest that pharmacological or psychological treatments aimed against repetition of deliberate self-harm (DSH) are effective. Furthermore, it should be borne in mind that a large proportion of individuals – particularly men – die as a result of their first suicide attempt. Strategies to reduce subsequent attempts should therefore be complemented by efforts to identify and treat those at risk of making an initial attempt.

TABLE 4.1

Useful questions when assessing the risk of suicide

• Do you think life is not worth living?

• Do you want to go to sleep and not wake up?

• Do you think having an accident would be a good thing?

• Have you had any thoughts of hurting yourself, or of suicide?

• Have you thought about how you might kill yourself?

• Have you made any definite plans to commit suicide?

Identification by the primary care physician

Both primary and secondary care physicians have an important role in identifying which individuals who have recently committed acts of DSH are at increased risk of suicide. There are over 100 000 cases of DSH in England and Wales each year, equivalent to about five people each year in a practice population of around 2500.

When compared with the general population, the risk of completed suicide is increased considerably in those who have recently harmed themselves and those with persisting suicidal thoughts. About 1–2% of all DSH patients commit suicide within 12 months of a previous suicide attempt, and about 16% make non-fatal suicide attempts within the same period.

There is no evidence that asking about suicide increases the risk of patient self-harm. By contrast, failing to ask about it may communicate an apparent lack of interest by the doctor, reinforcing a sense of rejection in the patient. When asking about suicidal thoughts or intent, it is usually sensible to adopt a sensitive but fairly direct approach, using a hierarchy of questions (Table 4.1). When accompanied by other factors

45

TABLE 4.2

Factors associated with increased suicide risk after acts of deliberate self-harm

- Act of deliberate self-harm planned long in advance
- Suicide note written
- Acts taken in anticipation of death (e.g. writing a will)
- Alone at the time of deliberate self-harm
- Efforts made to avoid discovery
- Did not seek help after deliberate self-harm
- Stated a wish to die
- Believed the act of deliberate self-harm would prove fatal
- Sorry the act of deliberate self-harm failed
- Continuing suicidal intent

suggesting a risk of further acts of DSH (Table 4.2), the presence of suicidal intent should cause significant concern, and the patient should usually be referred to specialist mental health services.

Identification within specialist mental health services

Up to 41% of suicide victims have received psychiatric inpatient care in the year prior to death, and up to 9% of suicide victims kill themselves within 1 day of discharge. It is difficult, however, to identify those at particular risk from within the general population of psychiatric inpatients; further research is required before targeted interventions can be recommended. At present, it seems that a history of DSH, suicidal thoughts noted while in hospital, and recent job loss or change in personal relationships are common among those at greatest risk of suicide within 12 months of discharge.

Suicide in hospital is, thankfully, a rare event; it is associated with male gender, previous DSH, compulsory admission to hospital, suicidal thoughts and absconding from the ward.

Individual risk factors often have low specificity or sensitivity, whereas changes in a cumulative risk may be more useful in predicting risk of suicide. If accurate identification of patients at particular risk becomes possible within the setting of standard clinical practice, then it may be possible to target measures to reduce the risk of death from suicide. Such measures may include the use of psychotropic drugs that are less toxic in overdose, or assertive outreach in the community after discharge from hospital.

Key points – suicide risk

- Depressed patients at particular risk of suicide include those with a history of deliberate self-harm, individuals with current suicidal thoughts and those who have recently been discharged from inpatient care.
- There is no evidence that asking about suicide increases the risk of patient self-harm.
- All depressed patients should be asked about the presence of suicidal thoughts, using a sensitive but direct approach.
- In the year after a suicide attempt, there is an increased risk for both further non-fatal self-harm (about 16% of patients) and completed suicide (about 1–2%).
- Patients with current suicidal intent should be referred to specialist mental health services.

Key references

Harris EC, Barraclough B. Suicide as an outcome for mental disorders. A meta-analysis. *Br J Psychiatry* 1997;170:205–28.

Hawton K, Arensman E, Townsend E et al. Deliberate self-harm: systematic review of efficacy of psychosocial and pharmaco-logical treatments in preventing repetition. *BMJ* 1998;317:441–7.

Hirschfeld RMA, Russell JM. Assessment and treatment of suicidal patients. *N Engl J Med* 1997;337:910–15.

Isometsa ET, Lonnqvist JK. Suicide attempts preceding completed suicide. *Br J Psychiatry* 1998;173:531–5.

King EA, Baldwin DS, Sinclair JMA et al. The Wessex Recent In-Patient Suicide Study, 1. Case-control study of 234 recently discharged psychiatric patient suicides. *Br J Psychiatry* 2001;178:531–6.

King EA, Baldwin DS, Sinclair JMA, Campbell MJ. The Wessex Recent In-Patient Suicide Study, 2. Case-control study of 59 in-patient suicides. *Br J Psychiatry* 2001;178:537–42.

McClure GMG. Changes in suicide in England and Wales, 1960–1997. *Br J Psychiatry* 2000;176:64–7.

Owens D, Horrocks J, House A. Fatal and non-fatal repetition of self-harm. Systematic review. *Br J Psychiatry* 2002;181:193–9.

Pirkis J, Burgess P. Suicide and recency of health care contacts: a systematic review. *Br J Psychiatry* 1998;173:462–74.

Unfortunately, depression is usually a recurring, and sometimes a chronic, condition. Epidemiological studies and prospective investigations reveal high rates of recurrence for both unipolar and bipolar depression; typically, 75% of patients will experience a second depressive episode within 10 years.

In patients with moderate or severe depressive episodes or dysthymia, antidepressant treatment is indicated. Patients who are reluctant to take antidepressant drugs should be considered for psychological treatments such as problem-solving, cognitive-behavioral or interpersonal therapy.

Unipolar depression

The risk of future episodes increases with each episode, as if some form of psychological or cerebral scarring has occurred. Typically, the length of the 'healthy' intervals shortens progressively, and disability increases and quality of life decreases with each new episode. There is also some evidence to suggest that the response to antidepressants decreases over time.

It is important to regard unipolar depression as a potentially lifelong condition. Hence, management should focus not only on acute treatment (i.e. getting ill patients well), but also on the long-term task of preventing early relapse or later recurrence of illness (i.e. keeping the patient well).

Epidemiological studies and investigations in clinical samples have shown that depressed patients have an excess of chronic physical symptoms (particularly pain), when compared with non-depressed controls, and these symptoms contribute to the burden of depression in the community.

Because most depressive episodes result from the combination of biological and psychosocial factors, the optimal treatment of depressed patients usually involves integrating psychological and physical treatment approaches with practical and emotional social support.

In primary care, medical treatment options are usually restricted to the prescription of antidepressant drugs. ECT is used occasionally by specialists; phototherapy (light treatment) may be helpful for some patients with SAD. Transcranial magnetic stimulation and vagus-nerve stimulation may eventually offer other physical treatment options, but the evidence for their efficacy remains rather limited. Furthermore, the inconvenience and costs preclude their widespread adoption as therapy for depressive illness.

Antidepressant drugs include the tricyclic antidepressants (TCAs) such as imipramine and amitriptyline, monoamine oxidase inhibitors (MAOIs) such as phenelzine, and the SSRIs citalopram, escitalopram, fluoxetine, fluvoxamine, paroxetine and sertraline; other compounds include the selective norepinephrine reuptake inhibitor reboxetine, and the dual-acting antidepressants (i.e. with effects on both serotonergic and norepinephine neurotransmission) duloxetine, venlafaxine, milnacipran (indicated in Japan, some parts of Europe and Latin America, but not in the UK or the USA) and mirtazapine.

Although the precise mechanism of action varies from drug to drug, all are presumed to work by increasing the availability of monoamines (typically, serotonin and/or norepinephrine) at the synapse, or through effecting changes in postsynaptic receptors. Many other potential antidepressant drugs are in development, some with novel mechanisms of action. These include antagonists at substance P receptors, corticotropin-releasing factor antagonists and drugs acting on melatonin receptors.

In standard practice, up to 65% of patients with moderate or severe depressive episodes will be substantially improved within 3 months of starting treatment. The response rate in major depression is similar in patients with or without preceding life events, and in those with or without comorbid medical illness.

Antidepressant drugs are not indicated for patients with acute, mild depression. Education, support and simple problem-solving may be all that is required, though patients should be reviewed to see whether they develop a more severe, major depression.

Efficacy and tolerability. Antidepressant drugs have similar overall efficacy in the majority of patients with depression, though SSRIs may be slightly less effective than TCAs in patients hospitalized for major depression, and MAOIs may be marginally more effective than TCAs in non-hospitalized patients with 'atypical' depression (characterized by somnolence, increased appetite and prominent anxiety).

Systematic reviews, meta-analyses and some, but not all, randomized controlled trials have suggested that antidepressants with a dual mechanism of action may be marginally more efficacious in some groups of patients (e.g. hospitalized patients or those with severe somatic symptoms), but the evidence is mixed and as yet inconclusive.

By continuing with antidepressants beyond symptomatic recovery, the risk of relapse can be halved, and longer-term treatment can prevent the emergence of new depressive episodes.

Unfortunately, many antidepressants fail to live up to the profile of the ideal agent (Table 5.1), with side effects limiting their use in some patients. Older drugs, such as the TCAs, may cause drowsiness and interfere with work, and can be dangerous when taken in overdose. TCAs should be avoided in patients with

TABLE 5.1

Characteristics of an 'ideal' antidepressant

- Effective across a wide range of depressive disorders
- Effective in short- and long-term treatment
- Rapid onset of action
- Suitable for once-daily dosage
- Effective across a wide range of age groups
- Well tolerated
- No behavioral toxicity
- Suitable for the medically ill
- Free from interactions with food or drugs
- Safe in overdose
- Inexpensive

cardiac disease, glaucoma and prostatomegaly; they should also be avoided if the individual is taking hypotensive drugs, because of the risk of falls. Newer drugs, such as the SSRIs, are better tolerated, much safer in overdose, and more likely than the older TCAs to be prescribed at therapeutic doses and for an adequate period of treatment. However, a recent meta-analysis found some evidence for the efficacy of TCAs at doses that have often been considered subtherapeutic. Furthermore, treatment-emergent sexual dysfunction can often occur with SSRI treatment.

The place of other antidepressants, such as venlafaxine, nefazodone, mirtazapine and reboxetine, in the overall treatment of patients with depression is still being evaluated.

Although newer antidepressants are more expensive than the older drugs, the currently available pharmacoeconomic data do not suggest that one drug or class should be favored over others for initial treatment, on the basis of cost alone.

Initiating treatment. When starting treatment with antidepressant drugs, it can be helpful to follow a fairly simple protocol (Table 5.2). Clearly, no two patients have identical problems, and clinical judgment is always required.

Discontinuing treatment. When any antidepressant drug is stopped abruptly, discontinuation symptoms may be experienced. Common symptoms include disturbance of balance and sensation, gastrointestinal upset and insomnia; typically, these arise within a few days and resolve a few weeks after stopping treatment. This pattern is different from that of relapsing depressive symptoms.

It seems sensible to taper the dose of antidepressant over 6 months in patients who have completed long-term maintenance

TABLE 5.2

Starting treatment with antidepressants

- Establish the presence of a treatable depressive disorder
- Exclude underlying severe mental disorder (e.g. schizophrenia)
- Determine the severity of depression
  - psychosis: refer to psychiatric services
  - severe: refer to psychiatric services
  - moderate: start an antidepressant
  - mild: review the patient later, consider referral for psychological treatments
- Establish whether general medical illness is present
- Choose an effective, well-tolerated, safe antidepressant
- Warn the patient about possible side effects
- Prescribe according to recommended practice
- Review adherence and side effects within 1 week
- Evaluate efficacy after about 4 weeks

treatment (e.g. after 5 years of successful maintenance). There is little evidence about the effects of tapering the dose when switching between different antidepressants.

Antidepressants with longer half-lives (e.g. fluoxetine) may be associated with fewer discontinuation symptoms than drugs with shorter half-lives (e.g. paroxetine and sertraline).

Psychological treatments. Many of the mildly depressed patients seen in primary care settings can be helped by simple support, and instruction in cognitive, behavioral or problem-solving techniques. However, moderately or severely ill patients generally require more intensive psychological approaches, such as a course of cognitive or interpersonal therapy.

The most effective psychological treatment approaches for depressed patients are those that are semi-manualized (i.e. conducted according to a treatment manual), relatively short term and focused on particular issues or problems. These directive, problem-focused, time-limited treatments are effective in the short term, and possibly have some value in delaying the onset of new depressive episodes.

Unfortunately, access to specialized psychological treatments is highly variable and often limited, sometimes with long waiting lists.

Cognitive-behavioral therapy (CBT) is one of the most extensively researched and widely adopted psychological treatments for depression. It is based on the observation that depressed patients make maladaptive assumptions about themselves and the outside world, and these color their processing of external events and alter their mood. Common examples of maladaptive assumptions include:

• I must try to please everybody all of the time
• it is wrong to get angry with those I love
• I must do well at everything I do.

Once activated, these assumptions lead to 'negative automatic thoughts', which arise without objective reason and lead to unpleasant emotional states, such as misery, anxiety or guilt. Depressed patients often consider themselves worthless, life to be meaningless and the future hopeless. In CBT, it is argued that these negative thoughts are the result of a number of typical processing errors through which perceptions of events are distorted. Examples of these processing errors include:

- selective abstraction, attending only to the negative aspects of an experience
- arbitrary inference, jumping to conclusions on inadequate evidence
- over-generalization, making judgments on the basis of single events.

During CBT, the therapist helps patients to identify their maladaptive assumptions and processing errors, and then to challenge them by monitoring their experience and associated emotional states. As 'homework', patients are asked to perform certain tasks, such as keeping a daily record of activities and listing negative thoughts as they occur. This is often complemented by behavioral techniques, such as scheduling pleasurable tasks and breaking seemingly insurmountable problems into smaller, achievable parts (Table 5.3).

Other psychosocial approaches that have been found to be helpful in primary and secondary care settings include interpersonal therapy, problem-solving treatment and social work intervention. Problem-solving treatment was found to be as effective in terms of symptom relief as amitriptyline treatment in a study of primary care patients with major depression, and was associated with higher levels of patient satisfaction and reduced dropout rates. In a second study in primary care, social

TABLE 5.3

Techniques used in cognitive-behavioral therapy for depression

- Keeping a daily record of activities and negative thoughts
- Monitoring negative thoughts associated with worsening of mood
- Challenging negative thoughts
- Using imagination to replay events
- Questioning the assumptions that lead to negative thoughts
- Planning rewarding activities throughout the day
- Praising oneself for achievements
- Dividing complex tasks into achievable components
- Visualizing performance in challenging situations

work intervention was more effective than standard primary physician care and as effective as amitriptyline treatment prescribed by a psychiatrist, and was also associated with a greater degree of patient satisfaction.

St John's Wort. In some countries, many depressed patients are treated with St John's Wort (*Hypericum perforatum*), a herbal remedy. Consumers also take it for a wide range of conditions, including or arising from insomnia, stress, bereavement and premenstrual syndrome. A review of clinical trials suggests that *Hypericum perforatum* is no more effective than placebo in the treatment of patients with depression of mild or moderate intensity.

Many patients are attracted to the preparation because of its natural origins and presumed safety, though different formulations vary in the bioavailability of the active principle (which has some SSRI-like properties). However, *Hypericum perforatum* preparations have been implicated in untoward drug interactions, and are best avoided while patients are being prescribed certain psychotropic drugs, such as SSRIs.

Self-help. Many patients derive considerable support from involvement in local self-help groups for depression, such as those run by Depression Alliance in the UK, or the Depression and Bipolar Support Alliance in the USA (see Useful resources, page 77). As well as providing information, understanding and support, group members can share useful tactics for coping with individual problems such as insomnia or loss of energy, and interpersonal problems arising from irritability or withdrawal. Many groups encourage the development of cognitive-behavioral skills and problem-solving techniques.

Treatment of depression in children and adolescents. There is much less evidence for the efficacy of treatment of depression in young people, compared with adults. A systematic review of CBT found it to be superior to other therapies (including supportive psychotherapy) in resolving depressive symptoms. However, CBT is a limited resource, and few primary care physicians have the necessary training in this therapy.

There has been much recent interest in the balance of risk and benefit when treating children or adolescents with SSRI antidepressants. Although a number of placebo-controlled trials have shown that antidepressants are efficacious in the treatment of childhood or adolescent major depressive disorder, clinical trial databases with some antidepressants suggest there may be a slightly increased risk of self-harm, usually in the first few weeks of treatment. The UK Committee on Safety of Medicines recommended (in early December 2004) that venlafaxine, mirtazapine and SSRIs (except fluoxetine) should not be used for the treatment of depressive illness in those aged under 18 years. In the USA, the FDA in March 2004 asked manufacturers of SSRIs and other newer generation antidepressants to include stronger cautions and warnings about monitoring patients for worsening of depression and suicidal ideation. As the pharmacokinetics of antidepressants appear similar in adolescent and adult patients, the doses prescribed for adolescents are often similar to those used in adults. In children, greater caution is required.

Bipolar affective disorder

The optimal pharmacological treatment for bipolar depression is unclear, but probably involves the combination of a mood-stabilizing drug and a short course of an antidepressant.

It is usually advisable to admit patients with manic episodes to hospital, as even the less severe (hypomanic) episodes are usually disruptive, and can lead to impulsive and reckless behavior or financial destitution. Considerable nursing skill is required to settle the euphoric manic patient, who is often overactive and sometimes lacking in insight.

The acute treatment of mania usually involves lithium, valproate or antipsychotic drugs, sometimes in combination. Antipsychotic drugs have an earlier onset of action, but conventional neuroleptics are less well tolerated than other treatments. Lithium and valproate are more often used as prophylactic treatments to reduce the risk of future manic or depressive episodes. Data are accumulating on the value of atypical antipsychotic drugs in maintenance treatment.

Lithium. When prescribed rationally, and when taken regularly, lithium can have startling effects, improving the course of the illness dramatically. It may also decrease the excess overall mortality associated with bipolar illness (reducing accident rates and the incidence of cardiovascular events) and may reduce suicide rates. However, many patients will derive little or no benefit from lithium, experiencing only the common side effects of thirst, tremor and weight gain. Treatment with lithium may precipitate or worsen skin problems, as well as causing leukocytosis and mild impairment of attention and memory. In addition, hypothyroidism and non-toxic goiter occur in about 5% and impaired renal tubular function occurs in 5–10% of patients undergoing long-term treatment. Use during pregnancy is associated with teratogenic effects in up to 11% of births, cardiovascular malformations being common.

Randomized controlled trials with lithium have found that it is effective in 60–90% of acutely ill patients with mania, and in up to 80% of patients when used in the prophylaxis of bipolar disorder. Although effective in the prophylaxis of unipolar depression, the efficacy of lithium in this indication is not as good as that of antidepressant drugs. Unfortunately, the good results seen with lithium in patients participating in treatment studies are often not replicated in routine clinical practice, where lithium therapy is not always undertaken in a rigorous way (there may be under-dosage, poor supervision and/or patient non-compliance). Treatment can be improved through the development of local protocols for care and specialized 'lithium clinics'.

In bipolar illness, the best results with lithium treatment are achieved when compliance is good, there is a family history of bipolar illness and when the pattern of affective episodes is of mania followed by depression. Results are not as good in the presence of rapid cycling illness, coexisting paranoid features and comorbid substance abuse.

Anticonvulsant drugs can be effective in patients who respond only partially to treatment with lithium, or in those with particularly rapid cycling affective disorder or mixed affective episodes. There is good evidence for using sodium valproate or carbamazepine in the acute treatment of mania and in the longer-term treatment of rapid cycling bipolar disorder. Evidence is accumulating to support the prophylactic use of these drugs in patients with bipolar illness, and both have been found helpful as adjuvants to lithium treatment.

Sodium valproate was first used in the treatment of primary generalized epilepsy, generalized absences and myoclonic seizures, but has also been found to be effective in treatment-refractory mania and rapid cycling bipolar disorder, particularly in non-psychotic patients. Until recently, there was limited evidence to support any prophylactic benefit, and valproate was reserved for adjunctive treatment. However, controlled trials have now shown that long-term treatment with valproate can prevent episodes of affective illness from occurring.

The adverse effects of valproate preparations include nausea and vomiting, hair loss, blood dyscrasias and hepatotoxicity; full blood counts and liver function tests should be performed regularly during treatment. Interactions may occur with certain antidepressant and antipsychotic drugs, and with antimalarials. Like lithium, valproate is potentially teratogenic, causing abnormalities of the heart, neural tube, lip and palate; it should be used with great caution during pregnancy.

Carbamazepine. The adverse effects of carbamazepine include headache and drowsiness, nausea and vomiting, blood dyscrasias and skin rashes, abnormal liver function tests, hepatitis and cholestatic jaundice. Like valproate and lithium, it has teratogenic effects, possibly as a consequence of folate deficiency.

Carbamazepine induces the metabolism of anticoagulants, certain antidepressant and antipsychotic drugs, oral contraceptives and steroids. In addition, there is a risk of interactions with alcohol, analgesics, antibacterials, calcium-channel blockers and ulcer-healing drugs. Because of these various adverse effects, carbamazepine is used less often than other anticonvulsants, though some patients respond preferentially to it.

Lamotrigine. The anticonvulsant lamotrigine has antidepressant properties, both in patients with epilepsy and in those with bipolar disorder. In the long-term treatment of bipolar disorder, it appears to be more efficacious than lithium in preventing new depressive episodes, whereas lithium is more efficacious in preventing episodes of mania or hypomania.

Psychological approaches. Although not yet studied extensively, the available evidence suggests self-management approaches are effective in the long-term treatment of patients with bipolar illness. These approaches incorporate heightened mood awareness, identification of prodromal symptoms, the acquisition of appropriate assertiveness, and spacing apart of activities and life events.

CBT appears to be more efficacious in patients without substance abuse comorbidity and in those with fewer previous episodes of illness.

Dysthymia

Patients with chronic mild depression can make considerable use of healthcare resources and often receive prescriptions of psychotropic drugs, but the treatment of dysthymia has not been investigated as extensively as that of other depressive disorders. Furthermore, there are flaws in the design and/or analysis of many early published studies of the treatment of dysthymic patients.

In recent consensus statements on the treatment of depressive illness, such as that produced by the British Association for

Fast Facts – Depression

Psychopharmacology, the recommendations for the treatment of dysthymia are very similar to those for major depression. Benefits have been described with imipramine, certain SSRIs (sertraline and fluoxetine) and moclobemide – particularly in patients with so-called 'double depression', in whom depressive episodes complicate an underlying dysthymic disorder.

Focused psychotherapies, such as CBT, may improve social functioning rather than improving depressive symptoms. Therefore, it seems sensible to offer a combined approach, using both antidepressant drugs and focused psychotherapy, to optimize clinical outcomes in dysthymic patients.

Postnatal depression

Many women with postnatal depression are reluctant to take antidepressant drugs, and the available evidence suggests that brief psychological therapy is often effective in mothers with moderate depression. Randomized controlled trials of non-directive counseling and instruction in cognitive-behavioral skills show that both are superior to routine care.

Antidepressant drugs are useful in women with more severe depression, and in those who have not responded to counseling. There is little evidence that combining anti-depressants with a psychological intervention increases efficacy above that achieved with either treatment when given alone.

All antidepressant drugs are secreted in breast milk, but plasma concentrations of TCAs and SSRIs in both mother and child are rarely detectable on standard assays. However, the baby should be watched carefully for possible unwanted effects, such as sedation. Estrogens may help some women with postnatal depression, but this approach is unlicensed and experimental, carries the risk of thromboembolism and is contraindicated in women who wish to breastfeed.

Recurrent brief depression

RBD has been formally recognized in only the last decade, and as yet no effective treatment has been established. It is probably misguided to attempt to manage acute depressive episodes with psychotropic drugs, as the episode will usually have resolved before any agent has become effective.

Double-blind placebo-controlled studies of fluoxetine, paroxetine, imipramine and moclobemide have not found any evidence that drug treatment reduces the frequency, severity or duration of individual episodes. Similarly, no forms of psychological treatment can be recommended, as no formal studies of psychotherapeutic approaches in RBD have been undertaken. Training in problem-solving skills may be of some value in preventing repetition of DSH, and could be helpful in the overall management of some patients with RBD. It seems sensible to advise patients to limit their alcohol consumption, and possibly to avoid the use of benzodiazepines.

'Resistant' depression

The long-term outcome for patients with depression is not as favorable as was initially thought; 20–35% of patients do not recover fully from a depressive episode, though full recovery is possible even after 10 years of depressive illness. A number of factors predict chronicity in depression, including demographic status (elderly, female), type of illness ('double depression', psychotic depression), comorbid physical illness and mental disorder, a positive family history and an anxiety-prone premorbid personality. Other factors include a delay in starting treatment, inappropriate or suboptimal treatment, poor compliance and therapeutic nihilism.

The management of resistant depression is usually a complex and time-consuming task, and is probably best left to specialist mental health services. However, primary care physicians may

TABLE 5.4

When depressed patients do not respond to treatment

- Confirm the diagnosis of a depressive disorder
- Exclude underlying mental disorders such as schizophrenia or dementia
- Establish whether maintaining factors are present (e.g. alcohol abuse)
- Perform a full physical examination
- Review the dosage of antidepressants
- Review the duration of treatment
- Ascertain whether the patient has adhered to treatment
- Withdraw depressogenic drugs, such as alcohol or benzodiazepines
- Advise a brief treatment washout period
- Change to another antidepressant
- Review the patient regularly over 6 weeks
- Refer if the patient remains depressed

wish to follow some simple steps before referral (Table 5.4). Combining antidepressants with psychological approaches based on CBT may represent the best approach for patients with chronic depression (i.e. of more than 2 years' duration).

Research into resistant depression has been hampered by the lack of official consensus as to what constitutes resistance. A number of double-blind placebo-controlled studies have been performed, using a variety of treatment approaches. The quality of these studies is highly variable; a recent systematic review found only 16 high-quality trials. Typically, about 50% of patients improve (but do not necessarily recover) with adjuvant treatments, including lithium, carbamazepine, L-tryptophan and liothyronine. Combining antidepressants from different classes can also be helpful, but is potentially hazardous and should be left to specialists.

Long-term treatment

Both unipolar depression and bipolar affective disorder should be regarded as potentially lifelong, episodic conditions. As such, the focus of treatment is shifting towards long-term management, designed to minimize the risks of early relapse and later recurrence of affective illness. The efficacy of many antidepressants, and some psychological therapies, in continuation and prophylactic treatment has been evaluated and most have been found to be beneficial. However, there is currently no good evidence to support the long-term use of nortriptyline or mianserin.

When used as maintenance treatment, the antidepressant should be prescribed at the dose that was successful in acute treatment. In patients experiencing a first depressive episode, the consensus is that antidepressants should be continued for at least 6 months after symptomatic recovery. There is still some uncertainty about the duration of prophylactic treatment in recurrent unipolar depression, though treatment should certainly be continued for at least 5 years and possibly indefinitely. The situation is less clear for bipolar depression, as extending the duration of antidepressant treatment can sometimes precipitate hypomanic or manic episodes, or even contribute to cycle acceleration, in which episodes of illness become more frequent over time. Antidepressant drugs should be used in bipolar patients only if they are also taking mood-stimulating drugs such as lithium or anticonvulsants.

Interpersonal therapy has some efficacy in preventing recurrence of depression, although it appears to be less efficacious than continuing with antidepressants. Recent findings in patients with chronic depression indicate that a simplified psychological treatment based on cognitive therapy is as efficacious as the antidepressant nefazodone, while combination treatment is significantly more efficacious than either treatment given alone.

Key points – treating depressive illness

- Antidepressant treatment is indicated in patients with moderate or severe depressive episodes or dysthymia.
- In patients experiencing their first depressive episode, antidepressant treatment should be continued for 6 months after resolution of symptoms; patients with recurrent depressive episodes usually need treatment for much longer (5 years or more).
- Patients who are reluctant to take antidepressant drugs should be considered for psychological treatments such as problem-solving, cognitive-behavioral therapy (CBT) or interpersonal therapy.
- The optimal pharmacological treatment for bipolar depression is unclear, but probably involves the combination of a mood-stabilizing drug and a short course of an antidepressant.
- Combining antidepressants with psychological approaches based on CBT may represent the best approach for patients with chronic depression (i.e. of more than 2 years' duration).

Key references

American Psychiatric Association (APA). Practice guideline for the treatment of patients with major depressive disorder. 2nd edn. In: *Practice Guidelines for the Treatment of Psychiatric Disorders. Compendium 2002.* Washington DC: APA, 2002:463–545.

Anderson IM, Nutt DJ, Deakin JFW. Evidence-based guidelines for treating depressive disorders with antidepressants: a revision of the 1993 British Association for Psychopharmacology guidelines. *J Psychopharmacol* 2000;14:3–20.

Appleby L, Warner R, Whitton A, Faragher B. A controlled study of fluoxetine and cognitive-behavioural counselling in the treatment of postnatal depression. *BMJ* 1997;314:932–6.

Donoghue J. Sub-optimal use of tricyclic antidepressants in primary care. *Acta Psychiatr Scand* 1998;98:429–31.

Dowrick C, Buchan I. Twelve month outcome of depression in general practice: does detection or disclosure make a difference? *BMJ* 1995;311:1274–6.

Frank E, Kupfer DJ, Perel JM et al. Three-year outcomes for maintenance therapies in recurrent depression. *Arch Gen Psychiatry* 1990;47:1093–9.

Furukawa TA, McGuire H, Barbui C. Meta-analysis of effects and side effects of low dosage tricyclic antidepressants in depression: systematic review. *BMJ* 2002;325:991–5.

Keller MB, McCullough JP, Klein DN et al. A comparison of nefazodone, the cognitive-behavioral analysis system of psychotherapy, and their combination for the treatment of chronic depression. *N Engl J Med* 2000;342:1462–70.

Mynors-Wallis LM, Gath DH, Lloyd-Thomas AR, Tomlinson D. Randomised controlled trial comparing problem solving treatment with amitriptyline and placebo for major depression in primary care. *BMJ* 1995;310: 441–5.

National Institute for Clinical Excellence (NICE). *Depression: management of depression in primary and secondary care.* Clinical Guideline 23 developed by the National Collaborating Centre for Mental Health. London: NICE, December 2004. www.nice.org.uk/ pdf/CG023NICEguideline.pdf

Rosenbaum JF, Fava M, Hoog SL et al. Selective serotonin reuptake inhibitor discontinuation syndrome: a randomized clinical trial. *Biol Psychiatry* 1998;44: 77–87.

Scott AIF, Freeman CPL. Edinburgh Primary Care Depression Study: treatment outcome, patient satisfaction and cost after 16 weeks. *BMJ* 1992;304:883–7.

Stimpson N, Agrawal N, Lewis G. Randomised controlled trials investigating pharmacological and psychological interventions for treatment-refractory depression. Systematic review. *Br J Psychiatry* 2002;181:284–94.

There has been considerable research into the treatment of anxiety disorders in the past decade. As a result, doctors may now be uncertain which treatment options should be considered 'first-line' approaches, and which should be reserved for patients who do not respond to initial therapy. Recent treatment guidelines have helped to clarify this situation (Table 6.1).

As with depression, anxiety disorders should be regarded as potentially lifelong conditions that are likely to require long-term treatment. Newer antidepressants (principally SSRIs) have proven efficacy in the acute and longer-term treatment of a broad range of anxiety disorders. Benzodiazepines should be reserved for patients who do not respond to antidepressant drugs, although short courses (1–2 weeks) may be beneficial while waiting for the efficacy of antidepressants to develop.

More detailed discussion of the therapeutic options for different coexisting anxiety disorders is given below.

Generalized anxiety disorder

The need for definitive treatment in generalized anxiety disorder depends on the severity of symptoms, the degree of personal distress, the level of occupational and social impairment and the patient's usual coping strategies.

Medical options. Benzodiazepines are effective anxiolytic drugs, but can cause troublesome sedation and have considerable potential for dependency; they must be prescribed with care. Relatively short courses (for less than 1–2 months) are usually appropriate during periods when the patient is particularly

TABLE 6.1

Recommendations for pharmacological treatment of anxiety disorders (based on guidelines produced by the World Federation of Societies of Biological Psychiatry)

Disorder	First-line agents	Second-line agents	Third-line agents
Generalized anxiety disorder	Venlafaxine SSRIs	Imipramine Buspirone	Unclear
Panic disorder	SSRIs (TCAs)	Benzodiazepines Phenelzine	Moclobemide, nefazodone, valproate, ondansetron
Social phobia	SSRIs	Phenelzine Moclobemide Benzodiazepines	Venlafaxine, nefazodone, gabapentin, pregabalin
Post-traumatic stress disorder	SSRIs	Amitriptyline Imipramine Phenelzine	Unclear
Obsessive–compulsive disorder	SSRIs	Clomipramine	Augmentation with haloperidol, risperidone (or lithium)

SSRIs, specific serotonin reuptake inhibitors; TCAs, tricyclic antidepressants.
Based on guidelines published in Bandelow B et al. 2002.

distressed or disabled by anxiety symptoms, and also at certain stages in a clear management plan. Other drugs found to be effective in randomized controlled trials include venlafaxine, certain TCAs, the SSRIs paroxetine, escitalopram and sertraline, and buspirone, none of which has the same potential for psychological or physical dependence as the benzodiazepines.

69

Psychological treatment. Management of patients with generalized anxiety disorder can also involve a range of psychological treatments. Problem-solving treatment, similar to that used in depression, has been developed and can be readily taught to patients by non-specialists.

More specialized forms of psychotherapy can be helpful for patients with more severe symptoms; these include applied relaxation, anxiety management training and CBT. A meta-analysis of CBT studies indicates that this approach is helpful in both the short and long term, though follow-up data are sparse. Relaxation training is usually more effective if taught by a nurse or therapist than if learned from a tape, but must be practised regularly to be beneficial.

Unfortunately, these more sophisticated forms of psychological treatment are not generally available in most clinical services and, where they are, waiting lists are often long. Drug treatment and simpler measures (e.g. anxiety management and relaxation training) are often used initially, with specialist psychological treatments being reserved for those patients who do not respond or who have a reluctance to try pharmacological approaches.

Panic disorder

The short-term goals for treatment of panic disorder include inducing a complete recovery from panic attacks, resolving anticipatory anxiety (i.e. fearful expectation of panic attacks) and any associated phobic avoidance, and treating any comorbid conditions. Preventing relapse and improving social and occupational function are important considerations for long-term management strategies.

Medical options. High-potency benzodiazepines (e.g. alprazolam) are effective in many patients, but can cause sedation and carry a risk of dependency. Various antidepressant drugs (SSRIs, imipramine, clomipramine) have been found to be helpful and are as effective as benzodiazepines in reducing anxiety symptoms, lessening agoraphobia and minimizing overall impairment; they are more beneficial than benzodiazepines in reducing associated depressive symptoms. SSRIs are generally considered to be the most favorable first-line treatment. Low initial doses of antidepressants are often necessary, as patients with panic disorder can be exquisitely sensitive to adverse effects of medication.

Psychological treatment. Certain psychological approaches are effective in the short-term treatment of panic disorder with or without agoraphobia. It is often necessary to begin treatment by helping patients to understand that their symptoms are not caused by serious physical disease, and that any fears of collapse or death are unfounded.

As with generalized anxiety disorder, relaxation training and problem-solving techniques can be helpful, but severely ill patients are most likely to benefit from more specialized psychological treatments, such as CBT, with or without graded exposure to any feared situations. Exposure therapy can be carried out under the supervision of a behavioral therapist or community psychiatric nurse, or by the patient in homework sessions.

Outcome. Follow-up studies continued for up to 20 years have shown that the long-term outcome in panic disorder is often poor – fewer than half of these patients become panic free, even after many years of treatment. It appears that some antidepressant drugs (e.g. paroxetine, sertraline) can help to prevent relapse after successful acute treatment, as can CBT; however, these long-term approaches have not been studied extensively.

Specific phobia

Patients with specific phobias are usually treated using behavioral therapy based on graded in-vivo exposure. Additional cognitive techniques are sometimes used, but probably contribute little to the efficacy of treatment. Approximately 75% of patients achieve substantial improvements, often after very few treatment sessions; there is some evidence that therapist-directed exposure is more effective than self-directed exposure. Medication is used only very occasionally, in patients who have not benefited from behavioral and cognitive techniques.

Patients with a specific fear of blood or bodily injury tend to develop bradycardia and hypotension when exposed to fearful stimuli. They therefore require tension exercises in addition to exposure therapy in order to gain optimal benefit from treatment.

Social phobia

Patients with social phobia can benefit from pharmacological treatments and cognitive-behavioral approaches, either alone or in combination. Although β-blockers are useful in the management of performance anxiety, they have little value in treating the generalized subtype of social phobia. Short-term treatment with alprazolam or clonazepam is helpful, but the risk of dependence argues against long-term use. Placebo-controlled studies have shown all of the following drugs to be effective in treating patients with social phobia: the traditional MAOI phenelzine; the newer reversible inhibitor of monoamine oxidase-A moclobemide; gabapentin and pregabalin (anticonvulsants); the SSRIs escitalopram, paroxetine, sertraline and fluvoxamine; and venlafaxine.

CBT (either individual or group-based) is helpful in many patients with social phobia, particularly when accompanied by in-vivo exposure. Group-based CBT may be more effective than certain antidepressants (e.g. phenelzine) for preventing relapse after symptomatic recovery. Somewhat surprisingly, social skills training does not appear to be helpful for patients with social phobia.

Key points – treating coexisting anxiety disorders

- Newer antidepressants (principally, selective serotonin reuptake inhibitors) have proven efficacy in the acute and longer-term treatment of a broad range of anxiety disorders.
- Benzodiazepines should be reserved for patients who do not respond to antidepressant drugs, although short courses (1–2 weeks) may be beneficial while waiting for the efficacy of antidepressants to develop.
- Patients with comorbid severe anxiety and depression would probably benefit from referral to specialist mental health services.
- As with depression, anxiety disorders should be regarded as potentially lifelong conditions that are likely to require long-term treatment.

Key references

Bandelow B, Zohar J, Hollander E et al. World Federation of Societies of Biological Psychiatry (WFSBP) guidelines for the pharmacological treatment of anxiety, obsessive–compulsive and post-traumatic stress disorders. *World J Biol Psychiatry* 2002;3:171–99.

Blanco C, Raza MS, Schneier FR, Liebowitz MR. The evidence-based pharmacological treatment of social anxiety disorder. *Int J Neuropsychopharmacol* 2003; 6:427–42.

Depression is the cause of considerable personal distress, increased morbidity and mortality, and troublesome interpersonal relationships. Furthermore, the burden of depression on society constitutes a major public health issue, despite the development of effective and more widely acceptable treatments.

Although common and often serious, depression is frequently overlooked by doctors and, in general, is managed quite poorly. The symptoms and signs of depression are probably associated with changes in both neuroendocrine status and neurotransmitter function, which should be normalized.

Potential new antidepressants

The next decade will undoubtedly see the arrival of new classes of antidepressant drugs, such as corticotropin-releasing factor antagonists, substance P antagonists, vasopressin-receptor antagonists and melatonin-receptor agonists. In addition, modifications to existing molecules, such as new formulations of bupropion, mirtazapine and selegiline, may offer the prospect of improved tolerability or an earlier onset of action, when compared with existing preparations.

Genetics

In recent years, it seemed that advances in the treatment of depression would outstrip increases in our understanding of the etiology and pathophysiology of the condition. However, considerable progress has now been made in identifying the possible neurobiology of depression, and knowledge of the human genome should soon improve our understanding of possible genetic predispositions to affective disorder. In addition, the developing science of pharmacogenomics should eventually lead to pharmacological treatment approaches that are tailored to particular subgroups of depressed patients.

Environmental aspects

Depressive syndromes probably represent the outward clinical expression of the progressive accumulation of genetic inheritance, particular patterns of early development, adversity in childhood, adolescence and early adult life, the experience of loss and environmental challenge. Research into the childhood antecedents of adult illness, and the differences in individual vulnerability and resilience, will therefore need to continue, complementing the more biological investigative approaches.

Enhancing existing treatment approaches

Although all these factors and variables require further investigation, much benefit would be gained from better use of the existing pharmacological treatments and increased availability of particular psychological therapies.

In primary care, instruction in the recognition of depression needs to be accompanied by advice about better use of evidence-based treatment. Greater overall benefit could be achieved by effective treatment of the already identified, more severely ill patients than by the ineffective treatment of newly recognized patients who are not so ill.

Treatment guidelines and algorithms offer the prospect of improved and more systematic treatment of depressed patients. However, it seems that guidelines alone are insufficient to provide improved clinical outcomes. Optimal results are seen when guidelines and education are combined with 'case management', in which there is individual responsibility (through a primary care physician or case worker) for assessing efficacy of treatment, adherence to treatment by the patient and adherence to the treatment protocol by the physician.

In secondary care, more concerted efforts are required to evaluate the effects of treatment and to prevent suicide, the latter being particularly pressing because of the apparent rise in the prevalence of depression in men and in adolescents. The gradual aging of the general population gives rise to more elderly depressed patients, so more efforts are needed to develop psychological treatments and antidepressant drugs that are effective and acceptable to this group.

In long-term management, pharmacological and psychological treatment approaches should be combined on the basis of objective assessment of the available evidence, rather than via the lottery of what is readily available. As certain patients appear to respond preferentially or react adversely to particular classes of antidepressant drugs, the discipline of personality assessment may experience something of a renaissance. Of course, these changes in professional practice need to be accompanied by continuing public education initiatives, designed to improve understanding of depression and hence to reduce the stigma associated with this disorder.

Key references

Baldwin DS, Thompson CV. The future of antidepressant pharmacotherapy. *World Psychiatry* 2003;2:3–8.

Von Korff M, Goldberg D. Improving outcomes in depression. *BMJ* 2001;323:948–9.

Useful resources

Self-help organizations

Association for Post Natal Illness (UK)
145 Dawes Road
Fulham, London SW6 7EB
Helpline: +44 (0)20 7386 0868
(Mon/Wed/Fri 10AM–2PM;
Tues/Thurs 10AM–5PM)
info@apni.org
www.apni.org

Cruse Bereavement Care (UK)
(Support and information following bereavement)
Cruse House, 126 Sheen Road
Richmond, Surrey TW9 1UR
Tel: +44 (0)20 8939 9530
Helpline: 0870 167 1677
Fax: +44 (0)20 8940 7638
helpline@crusebereavementcare.org.uk
www.crusebereavementcare.org.uk

Depression Alliance (UK)
212 Spitfire Studios
63–71 Collier St., London N1 9BE
Tel: 0845 123 2320
wales@depressionalliance.org
info@dascot.org
www.depressionalliance.org

Depression and Bipolar Support Alliance (USA)
730 N. Franklin St., Suite 501
Chicago, IL 60610-7224
Tel: 800 826 3632
Fax: +1 312 642 7243
www.dbsalliance.org

Manic Depression Fellowship (UK)
Castle Works
21 St George's Road
London SE1 6ES
Tel: 08456 340 540
Fax: +44 (0)20 7793 2639
mdf@mdf.org.uk
www.mdf.org.uk

Mental Health Foundation (UK)
20 Upper Ground
London SE1 9QB
Tel: +44 (0)20 7803 1100
Fax: +44 (0)20 7803 1111
mhf@mhf.org.uk
www.mhf.org.uk

Relate (UK)
(Counseling for people in relationships)
Herbert Gray College
Little Church Street
Rugby, Warks CV21 3AP
Tel: 0845 456 1310 or
+44 (0)1788 573 241
enquiries@relate.org.uk
www.relate.org.uk

Samaritans (UK)
(Open 24 hours a day, every day of the year)
The Upper Mill, Kingston Road
Ewell, Surrey KT17 2AF
Tel: +44 (0)20 8394 8300
Helpline: 08457 90 90 90
Fax: +44 (0)20 8394 8301
admin@samaritans.org
www.samaritans.org.uk

Seasonal Affective Disorder
Association (UK)
PO Box 989
Steyning BN44 3HG
www.sada.org.uk

Information
National Electronic Library for
Mental Health (UK)
www.nelmh.org

UK Mental Health Resource Centre
www.ukmentalhealth.org.uk

Pharmacology
American College of
Neuropsychopharmacology
ACNP Executive Office
545 Mainstream Drive
Suite 110
Nashville, TN 37228
Tel: +1 615 324 2360
Fax: +1 615 324 2361
acnp@acnp.org
www.acnp.org

British Association for
Psychopharmacology
36 Cambridge Place
Hills Road
Cambridge CB2 1NS
Tel: +44 (0)1223 358 395
www.bap.org.uk

Useful websites on pharmacology
and evidence-based medicine
www.bnf.org
www.cebm.net
www.cponline.gsm.com
www.fda.gov
www.mca.gov.uk
www.medicines.org.uk
www.nettingtheevidence.org.uk
www.pharmweb.net

Professional organizations
American Foundation for Suicide
Prevention
120 Wall Street, 22nd Floor
New York, NY 10005
Tel: +1 212 363 3500
Toll free: 888 333 AFSP
Fax: +1 212 363 6237
inquiry@afsp.org
www.afsp.org

American Psychiatric Association
1000 Wilson Blvd, Suite 1825
Arlington, Virginia 22209-3901
Tel: +1 703 907 7300
apa@psych.org
www.psych.org

American Psychological
Association
750 First Street, NE
Washington, DC 20002-4242
Tel: 800 374 2721
www.apa.org

British Psychological Society
St Andrews House
48 Princess Road East
Leicester LE1 7DR
Tel: +44 (0)116 254 9568
Fax: +44 (0)116 247 0787
enquiry@bps.org.uk
www.bps.org.uk

International Brain Research
Association
255 rue Saint Honoré
F-75001 Paris, France
Tel: +33 (0)1 4647 9292
admin@ibro.info
www.ibro.org

National Alliance for the
Mentally Ill (USA)
Colonial Place Three
2107 Wilson Blvd, Suite 300
Arlington, VA 22201-3042
Tel: +1 (703) 524 7600
Helpline: 800 950 6264
Fax: +1 (703) 524 9094
www.nami.org

National Alliance for Research on
Schizophrenia and Depression
(USA)
60 Cutter Mill Road, Suite 404
Great Neck, New York
NY 11021
Tel: 800 829 8289
Fax: +1 516 487 6930
info@narsad.org
www.narsad.org

National Mental Health
Association (USA)
2001 N Beauregard Street
12th Floor, Alexandria
Virginia 22311
Tel: +1 703 684 7722
Toll free: 800 969 6642
Fax: +1 703 684 5968
www.nmha.org

National Pharmaceutical
Association (UK)
Mallinson House
38–42 St Peter's Street
St Albans, Herts AL1 3NP
Tel: +44 (0)1727 832161
Fax: +44 (0)1727 840858
npa@npa.co.uk
www.npa.co.uk

Royal College of Psychiatrists
17 Belgrave Square
London SW1X 8PG
Tel: +44 (0)20 7235 2351
Fax: +44 (0)20 7245 1231
rcpsych@rcpsych.ac.uk
www.rcpsych.ac.uk

Society of Biological
Psychiatry (USA)
Maggie Peterson
c/o Mayo Clinic Jacksonville
Research – Birdsall 310
4500 San Pablo Road
Jacksonville, Florida 32224
Tel: +1 904 953 2842
Fax: +1 904 953 7117
peterson.maggie@mayo.edu
www.sobp.org

Society for Neuroscience (USA)
11 Dupont Circle, NW
Suite 500
Washington, DC 20036
Tel: +1 202 462 6688
Fax: +1 202 462 9740
info@sfn.org
apu.sfn.org

World Federation of Societies of
Biological Psychiatry
Avenue de Tervueren, 300
B-1150 Brussels, Belgium
Tel: +32 (0)2 743 15 80
Fax: +32 (0)2 743 15 50
global.headquarters@wfsbp.org
www.wfsbp.org

World Psychiatric Association
Department of Psychiatry and
Behavioral Sciences
Metropolitan Hospital Center
New York Medical College
1901 First Avenue, Suite 4M-3
New York, NY 10029
Tel: +1 212 423 7001
Fax: +1 212 876 3793
wpasecretariat@wpanet.org
www.wpanet.org

Journal weblinks

Behavioural Pharmacology
www.behaviouralpharm.com

Current Opinion in Psychiatry
www.co-psychiatry.com

International Clinical
Psychopharmacology
www.intclinpsychopharm.com

International Journal of
Psychiatry in Clinical Practice
www.tandf.co.uk/journals/titles/
13651501.asp

Journal of Neuroscience
www.jneurosci.org

Journal of Psychiatry and
Neuroscience
www.cma.ca/jpn

Index